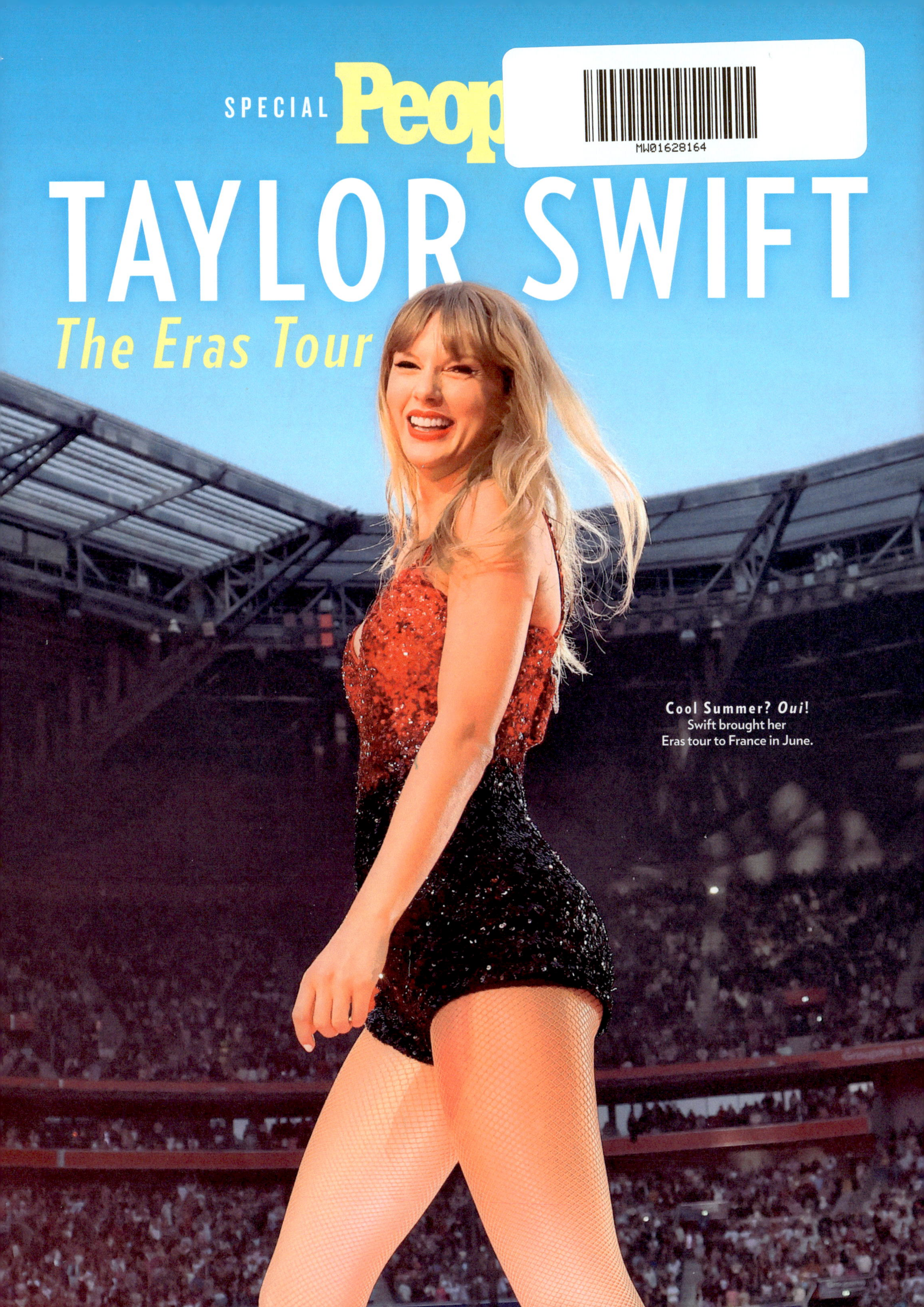

Cool Summer? *Oui*! Swift brought her Eras tour to France in June.

Out of This World In the newly added *Tortured Poets Department* segment Swift debuted in Paris, this projected UFO during "Down Bad" made for an OMG moment.

Contents

Look What You Made Me Do
A dapperly dressed Kelce (right) stunned Swifties with his London appearance to help the singer with a choreographed costume change, at one point carrying her to a sofa. "The one thing I told myself is, 'Do not drop the baby,'" he recalled afterward. "'Do not drop Taylor on your way over to this damn couch.'"

Thrill of a Lifetime

AROUND THE GLOBE, THE ERAS TOUR HAS BECOME A ONCE-IN-A-GENERATION EVENT. WELCOME TO WORLD DOMINATION (TAYLOR'S VERSION)

By **KEVIN O'DONNELL**

I swallowed a bug!" declared Taylor Swift, partway through her rendition of "All Too Well" at London's Wembley Stadium in June. As she recovered, she asked the crowd, "Can you sing?" (Boy, could they ever!) Mere seconds later she picked up where she left off.

Onstage—and off—Swift is unstoppable. Ever since she released her self-

'IT FEELS LIKE WE JUST PLAYED OUR FIRST SHOW . . . BECAUSE YOU HAVE MADE THIS SO FUN FOR US'

—TAYLOR SWIFT, ON THE 100TH NIGHT OF THE ERAS TOUR

titled debut album nearly two decades ago, she has obliterated all manner of music-industry records. Her colossal Eras tour—more than 150 dates spanning five continents—represents yet another jewel in her glitter-encrusted crown.

This special issue of *People* deep-dives into the global phenom, a 45-song celebration of the singer-songwriter's artistic evolution from Nashville upstart to chart-topping pop queen. It's the best seat in the house for the songs and scenery, the fashion and fun, including the new additions to the show taken from her latest album, *The Tortured Poets Department*. You'll also get a look at Taylor's life offstage, including her romance with NFL star Travis Kelce, who's spent more than a dozen nights cheering alongside other concertgoers. The bond between Swift and the Swifties remains unbreakable. When a thwarted alleged terror plot led to the cancellation of three Vienna shows in August, fans there poured into the streets to trade friendship bracelets and sing en masse: "You Need to Calm Down." Swift, devastated to let anyone down, quickly worked with Disney+ to make the Eras concert film available for free on Austrian TV.

Most musicians unveil a concert retrospective at the end of a career, not in the midst of a white-hot streak. And while the Eras tour has certainly dominated the pop culture conversation since launching in March 2023, it has also catapulted the star into something less quantifiable, though perhaps more significant: She has cemented herself as the most consequential artist of a generation. In a time when pop has become more fragmented than ever, she has single-handedly owned the culture. As the artist (and Swift pal) Phoebe Bridgers put it, "Beatlemania and *Thriller* have nothing on these shows."

The effort on Swift's part has been monumental. "It's taken over everything," she gleefully admitted from the stage in Liverpool in June. "I think I once had hobbies, but I don't know what they were anymore because all I do when I'm not onstage is sit at home and try to think of clever acoustic song mash-ups." And because of that tireless devotion we're all the richer.

The Eras Extravaganza

INSIDE THE TOUR

SLIP ON YOUR FRIENDSHIP BRACELETS, BREAK OUT YOUR SHINIEST SEQUINS, AND SETTLE INTO THIS FRONT-ROW SEAT FOR TAYLOR'S GREATEST SHOW ON EARTH

By **KEVIN O'DONNELL**

Giving Her All
Demand for the tour was unprecedented—the presale crashed Ticketmaster's website, while secondary sales for nosebleed seats cost thousands of dollars—but Swift ensured that every minute of the three-hour concert was worth it for her fans. "I wanted to play a show that was longer than they ever thought it would be," said the star (seen here in Edinburgh in June). "Because that makes me feel good leaving the stadium."

The Beat Goes On

In her updated shows (the first, in May at the La Défense Arena in Paris, above) Swift marches along with backing drummers for "The Smallest Man Who Ever Lived." Her taffeta Vivienne Westwood ball gown is adorned with the "Fortnight" lyric "I love you, It's ruining my life." At one point she tops the ensemble with a hussar military jacket featuring epaulet shoulders (below).

The *Tortured Poets Department* Era

A surprise addition to the show, this segment, set among a nearly all black-and-white color scheme, recalls Old Hollywood and showcases songs from Swift's most recent album, a 31-track opus. She performs before visuals that include a haunted house, alien spaceships and the asylum from the video to the hit lead single, "Fortnight."

Tortured Trappings

Set pieces and props for this era include a pair of "Fortnight" typewriters (above, left) and a rolling platform that evokes a 19th-century hospital bed, complete with *TTPD*-branded head- and baseboards (above). Feathered fans, top hats and tailcoats inject a vintage showbiz glitz into "I Can Do It With a Broken Heart" (below, left and below).

Swept Away
Swift rides a mirrored platform that reflects the stage-floor projections and slides around in a way that prompted fans to dub it "the Roomba."

'THAT WAS *THE TORTURED POETS DEPARTMENT* OR AS I LIKE TO CALL IT, FEMALE RAGE: THE MUSICAL'

—TAYLOR SWIFT, CONCLUDING THE SET ON MAY 9

The *Lover* Era

This set features songs from Swift's romantic 2019 synth-pop opus. Notably the inclusion of "Cruel Summer" in such a pivotal spot sent the song to the top of the *Billboard* Hot 100 a whole four years after its release. From the stage in Pittsburgh, Swift called this resurgence "the weirdest, most magical thing."

Fiscal Fitness

The economic effects of Swift's Eras tour have been massive. In the U.S., consumer spending related to her concerts is projected to be more than $5 billion, and the Fed has credited her with helping to revive tourism across the country. "If Taylor Swift were an economy," noted an economic analyst in GlobeNewswire, "she'd be bigger than 50 countries." No wonder dancer Whyley Yoshimura raises a toast to his Louboutin-booted boss during "The Man" (above).

A Meaningful Mansion
From her music videos to the emojis in her Instagram posts, Swift is famous for dropping Easter eggs for her fans. The massive Lover House (inspired by the titular music video) presents all sorts of innumerable clues for Swifties to parse. The most plausible meaning: Each room (including the front door) represents one of her studio albums.

The *Fearless* Era

The record that made Swift a household name gets a short but impactful slot in the show: When she performs the three key tracks ("Fearless," "You Belong With Me" and "Love Story"), the stadiums erupt into a joyous sing-along.

Standing Strong

To condition herself for the grueling show full of strumming, singing and dancing (all ably backed by, from left, Melanie Nyema, Kamilah Marshall and Eliotte Nicole), Swift would run on a treadmill while belting the set list. She also underwent three months of dance training with choreographer Mandy Moore (not the actress) and has been abstaining from alcohol. "I want to be so over-rehearsed that I could be silly with the fans," she told *Time*, "and not lose my train of thought."

Fringe Element
Swift (performing in Glendale, Ariz.) dons 16 different looks in the show, including pieces designed by Versace, Nicole + Felicia Couture, Alberta Ferretti and this ombré sequined look by Roberto Cavalli.

'THIS IS THE PROUDEST AND HAPPIEST I'VE EVER FELT AND THE MOST CREATIVELY FULFILLED AND FREE I'VE EVER BEEN'
—TAYLOR SWIFT

The *Evermore* Era

This portion of the evening is drawn from Swift's surprise 2020 album, made amid the coronavirus lockdown, during which she told Apple Music, "My world felt opened up creatively." It features some of the most intimate, stripped-back tunes of the show, including "Champagne Problems" and "Marjorie." Starting with the European leg of the tour, Swift merged the *Evermore* and *Folklore* eras, jokingly referring to the combo segment as "the Sister Albums."

Force of Nature
Swift re-created the moss-covered piano featured in her forest-set "Cardigan" music video. She described the woodland as a symbol of "the evergreen beginning of a relationship where everything seems magical and full of beauty."

Gold Rush

An Etro corset-top dress complemented this segment's homespun, rural aesthetic. Swift surprised fans at a Seattle show by inviting opening-act trio Haim onstage to perform their song "No Body, No Crime" for the first time together in concert (opposite). "Seattle…was genuinely one of my favorite weekends ever," Swift wrote on Instagram.

The *Reputation* Era

Swift's sixth album, which leans heavily on electronic production and hip-hop-style beats, may be her most misunderstood, but this four-song segment electrifies, including sultry renditions of "...Ready for It?" and "Look What You Made Me Do."

'[*REPUTATION*] IS A GOTH-PUNK MOMENT OF FEMALE RAGE AT BEING GASLIT BY AN ENTIRE SOCIAL STRUCTURE. I THINK A LOT OF PEOPLE SEE IT, AND THEY'RE JUST LIKE, "SICK SNAKES AND STROBE LIGHTS"'

—SWIFT, TO *TIME* IN 2023

Songbirds and Snakes

Following her very public feud with Kim Kardashian and Kanye West in 2016—after which Swift's social media comments were flooded with snake emojis by Kardashian stans—the pop star reclaimed the visual for *Reputation*. Snake imagery is smartly woven into the live show, from the beaded details on her bodice to an onstage shadow of Swift that morphs into a slithering serpent.

Poetry in Motion
Swift has good-naturedly downplayed her dancing skills—"Learning choreography is not my strong suit," she has said. For Eras, she surrounded herself with an army of 15 ace backup performers with impressive pedigrees that range from ex-ballet dancers and Rockettes to having past gigs supporting Janet Jackson and Jennifer Lopez.

The *Speak Now* Era

Swift released the rerecorded version of her 2010 album in the midst of her Eras tour and dropped several live surprises for fans, among them a premiere of the video for the track "I Can See You" during her July 2023 show in Kansas City, Mo.

'IT WAS JUST SO UNFATHOMABLY SPECIAL TO ME'
—SWIFT, ON PERFORMING THE *SPEAK NOW* SEGMENT IN KANSAS CITY, MO.

Pump Up the Volume
Swift and her stylist Joseph Cassell Falconer worked closely with designers to create big, bold iconic looks. "He gave us some direction and picked a few styles from our past collections that she loved," said Nicole + Felicia's Nicole Chang, "and then we made changes from those."

Frock Star
Nicole + Felicia designed many of the handcrafted gowns that Swift wears during the show, including the sequined halter-neck piece shown below. "[It's] a moment," creative director Nicole Chang told *People* of that dress. "Our head designer for evening[wear] spent days drawing out the pattern. He was in the office past midnight every day for a week or two."

The *Red* Era

The record where Swift morphed into an all-out pop superstar gets rowdy fist-pumping concert renditions of "We Are Never Ever Getting Back Together" and "I Knew You Were Trouble."

Vital Signs
Swift has rotated sequined T-shirts like these throughout the tour, and her fans—ever the forensic analysts—have speculated that the letters in red add up to coded messages. This shirt, worn in Arizona in March 2023, hinted at the release of *Speak Now (Taylor's Version)* four months later.

Awed Couples

While she often thrills Swifties with up-close interactions, Swift herself has been rendered starstruck when joined onstage by collaborators and pals including Phoebe Bridgers (below), whom she called a "boss genius angel baby face." In Nashville the pair performed "Nothing New," the song's live debut.

'I KNOW I'M GOING ON THAT STAGE WHETHER I'M SICK, INJURED, HEARTBROKEN, UNCOMFORTABLE OR STRESSED. THAT'S PART OF MY IDENTITY AS A HUMAN BEING NOW'
—SWIFT, TO *TIME* IN 2023

The *Folklore* Era

The cottage-core themes of her *Evermore* set list continue in the *Folklore* era, when Swift turns the stage into an intriguing bucolic fantasy worthy of the album's rustic feel.

Go With the Flow
Alberta Ferretti's chiffon gowns for Eras, including this midriff-revealing design with leaf embroidery, were intended to reflect the Italian-born designer's passion points, which she described to *Harper's Bazaar* as "lightness, femininity, romance, attention to detail and a delicate, gentle seduction."

'I KNEW THIS TOUR WAS HARDER THAN ANYTHING I'D EVER DONE BEFORE BY A LONG SHOT'
—SWIFT, TO *TIME* IN 2023

Risky Business

While performing in Tokyo, Swift nearly slipped off the roof of the cottage set (left), and during rainstorms in Foxborough, Mass., Swift performed her piano solos amid a downpour. "I feel like I'm in a water park," she joked.

The *1989* Era

The pop bangers return when Swift tears through songs from her Grammy-winning smash—the record where she fully broke free from her Nashville roots.

Joyride Swift's backup dancers do double duty as cyclists when they crisscross the stage on neon-lit bikes during "Blank Space."

Rainbow Bright
Roberto Cavalli creative director Fausto Puglisi, who also designed looks for Beyoncé's Renaissance tour, created these crop-top-and-skirt looks in several variations, including a cheeky take on the colors of the Kansas City Chiefs. "The more the better," he wrote on Instagram.

Travis
Shout-
Out!

The Acoustic Set

Unforeseen Circumstances

Swift often delivers fresh set-list additions and surprises during this segment of the show. One night in New Jersey she premiered the music video for her single "Karma" (above), and in Tampa she was joined by the National's Aaron Dessner for a rendition of "The Great War" (opposite).

Purple Reign
Oscar de la Renta designed several looks for Swift's tour, including this dazzling ensemble she dons during "Lavender Haze": a faux-fur coat with crystal embroidery and a sequin-embroidered T-shirt, which the company has dubbed "aurora borealis."

The *Midnights* Era

Swift closes out the show with picks from her 2022 effort, which she described as "the stories of 13 sleepless nights scattered throughout my life." With its rousing renditions of the chart-toppers "Anti-Hero" and "Karma," among others, blissful fans stay wide-awake.

Going Out in Style

For "Vigilante S---," Swift and her crew cavort on cafe chairs in homage to dance legend Bob Fosse (above). The singer caps the night with one of her most infectious (and biting) tunes: "Karma," which alludes to her dispute with Scooter Braun, who purchased (then sold) the master recordings to her first six albums. During the number, Swift glittered among confetti (below), and in New Jersey, Ice Spice—a guest collaborator on the song's remix—strutted alongside her (opposite).

Lights, Cameras, Action
Concertgoers film in a frenzy at Rio de Janeiro's Estádio Olímpico Nilton Santos, one of a trio of shows Swift performed in the Brazilian city.

IT'S A LOVE STORY, BABY

SCORES OF SWIFTIES FLOCKED TO STADIUMS ACROSS FIVE CONTINENTS, REVELING IN THEIR DEEP BOND WITH TAYLOR—AND THE STAR BEAMED THE ADORATION RIGHT BACK AT 'EM

gocase
Dare to dream
TAYLOR SWIFT
THE ERAS TOUR
VIP

Celebs in the Crowd

Hopelessly Devoted

Clockwise from above, left: *Stranger Things* star Maya Hawke caught Eras in Nashville; Julia Roberts took a selfie in Dublin; and Swift blew kisses from the stage in São Paulo, Brazil, to a young fan.

Standing Together
When three August concerts were canceled following a foiled alleged terror plot in Vienna, fans there gathered outside to sing Swift songs (including "All Too Well" and "You Need to Calm Down"), exchange friendship bracelets and adorn trees with them. "You can't break the spirit of Swifties," wrote an admirer on X (FKA Twitter). "This is girlhood. Turning something ugly into something beautiful."

The Royal Treatment
What a good dad! Prince William spent his 42nd birthday bringing kids George and Charlotte to Swift's June 21 London show. Backstage they posed for a selfie, which the Prince and Princess of Wales shared on their Instagram account, thanking the star "for a great evening!" She wrote back on hers: "Happy Bday M8!"

Every Time Travis Kelce Caught the Eras Tour—*So Far!*

The football star has popped up at 14 stops, trading bracelets and charming fans. "There won't be a bad show, I promise you that," he told *Entertainment Tonight*. "You know I gotta go support."

KANSAS CITY, MISSOURI
July 8, 2023

BUENOS AIRES, ARGENTINA
Nov. 11, 2023

SYDNEY, AUSTRALIA
Feb. 23, 2024
(pictured above)

SINGAPORE
Two dates in
March 2024

PARIS, FRANCE
May 12, 2024

LONDON, ENGLAND
June 21-23, 2024

DUBLIN, IRELAND
June 30, 2024

AMSTERDAM, THE NETHERLANDS
July 5-6, 2024

GELSENKIRCHEN, GERMANY
July 17-18, 2024

The Eras Tour BY THE NUMBERS

$55 MILLION
IN BONUSES GIVEN TO BACKUP PERFORMERS AND TOUR SUPPORT STAFF

Over $2 BILLION
IN PROJECTED TICKET SALES, AN ALL-TIME TOUR RECORD

2.3
MAGNITUDE OF AN EARTHQUAKE TRIGGERED BY FANS AT A SEATTLE SHOW

ONE
BUG SWALLOWED BY SWIFT ONSTAGE IN CHICAGO

2
BUGS NAMED AFTER HER: A MILLIPEDE (*NANNARIA SWIFTAE*) AND A SPIDER (*CASTIANEIRA SWIFTAY*)

28.9 TERABYTES
Amount of cell-phone data moved at an Arlington, Texas, show, the most AT&T moved at any stadium event in 2023

$2,675

COST OF THE TIFFANY DIAMOND WIRE RING SWIFT BEGAN WEARING AT THE JUNE 23RD SHOW (DO THE TWO "T"S STAND FOR TAYLOR & TRAVIS?)

3 HOURS

AVERAGE RUN TIME OF EACH SHOW

152

SHOWS WORLDWIDE

$93 MILLION (EST.)

SPENT BY FANS ON TICKETS, TRAVEL, FOOD, OUTFITS AND MERCH FOR EACH SHOW

NEARLY 8 MINUTES

OF CROWD APPLAUSE AND CHEERS AFTER "CHAMPAGNE PROBLEMS" IN LOS ANGELES

5,300

HAND-EMBROIDERED CRYSTALS AND BEADS ON THE OSCAR DE LA RENTA MIDNIGHT BODYSUIT

$4.1 BILLION

Swift's estimated personal earnings from the Eras tour, more than the yearly economic output of 42 countries

7:1

SCALE OF TAYLOR'S COSTUMES TO CUSTOM DUPES FOR BADGER THE CAT (@BADGER.DOT ON INSTA)

The Blissful Poet's Department

MAXIMIZING HER MOMENT

IT HASN'T BEEN ALL SET LISTS AND SPOTLIGHTS DURING THE TOUR—TAYLOR'S ALSO CARVED OUT PLENTY OF SPACE FOR FUN WITH FRIENDS, AN EPIC NEW ALBUM AND A RIVETING ROMANCE

ON A WINNING STREAK

SURELY IT'S NOT EASY BEING THE WORLD'S BIGGEST POP STAR. BUT WITH A LITTLE SUPPORT FROM HER SQUAD AND A HANDSOME NFL CHAMP, SWIFT HAS FOUND A WAY TO ENJOY EACH MOMENT AMID THE MAYHEM. SAID THE SINGER: 'MY LIFE FINALLY FEELS LIKE IT MAKES SENSE'

By **CHRIS NASHAWATY**

THE NUMBERS TELL AN ASTONISHING STORY: The Eras tour, which pulled in more than $1 billion across the U.S. and is projected to take in another billion by the time it wraps up in December, is already the highest-grossing global tour in history. As a live act, Taylor Swift has elbowed past a record-setting boys club of Elton John, the Rolling Stones, Ed Sheeran and U2. Filmed for posterity, Eras onscreen quickly racked up $261.7 million at the global box office to become the top-earning concert movie ever. That's got to be satisfying.

But life is not measured only in ledgers. Nor is it lived only on stages. (Though when you're Taylor Swift, every moment must feel that way.) So while the 34-year-old has spent the majority of her latest era performing to sold-out audiences under bright stadium lights, this period has also been marked by great off-stage creativity and evident joy. She delighted fans with a whopping 31-song album, *The Tortured Poets Department,* which became her 14th No. 1. And she continued to take control of her career on her own terms by rerecording *1989.* Doing things her way has been unquestionably profitable. But Swift's resulting world domination has had another less quantifiable effect: It has brought people together.

Continued on page 66

Love Field
Swift celebrated Travis Kelce's Super Bowl win with him on the grass right after the game. "I'm the happiest I've ever been," Kelce later told *People*. "My glass is all the way full."

Sunday Funday
The singer dined with Kelce at Manhattan's Waverly Inn in October 2023 following their appearances on *SNL* the previous night.

Tee Party
Right: Travis Kelce (with brother Jason, left) played in a celebrity golf tournament in Stateline, Nev., in July to the delight of some cheeky, politically minded Swifties (above).

Fest Dressed
Attending April's Coachella music festival outside Palm Springs, Calif., Swift rocked a skirt with a built-in garter, while Kelce boldly mixed plaid and stripes.

Shipshape
Left: At the Grammy Awards in February, country-pop singer Kelsea Ballerini puckered up with her lucky-in-love pal. Ballerini has said, "I adore Taylor. I adore Travis. So if they're happy, I ship it. Period."

Awe-Inspiring Artists
Opposite, top: Celine Dion (with son René-Charles Angélil) announced *Midnights* as Album of the Year. "It was an honor for me that they thought of me to present to Taylor Swift. It was [her] fourth [time] winning this award, which is exceptional," Dion told *People*.

Business Casual
Opposite, bottom: Friends and collaborators Lana Del Rey, Phoebe Bridgers, Swift and producer Jack Antonoff clowned around during a break in the show.

Continued from page 62

In the splintered and compartmentalized 21st century, global pop stars were thought to be a thing of the past. The age when all of us listened to the same music, saw the same movies and watched the same TV shows seemed dead and buried. We were told that we would all split off into our own separate little fan tribes in our own little corners of the Internet. There weren't supposed to be entertainers with broad appeal anymore. But Swift would not only prove that assumption wrong, she would also become the kind of rare commercial and cultural juggernaut we haven't seen since the days of Michael Jackson and the Beatles.

Swift showed us all that she was the ultimate multitasker, becoming a new kind of Hollywood powerhouse, a still-devoted ringleader of her beloved girl squad, and yes, she would even find time to start dating "the boy on the football team"—and not just any boy but an All-Pro tight end for the Kansas City Chiefs. It was an idyllic meet-cute fantasy straight out of one of her songs. Swift had, of course, been in high-profile relationships before she began dating Travis Kelce, but this time it seemed different. More natural, more relaxed. At least to those of us watching from the sidelines, which was basically everyone.

While the couple tried to keep the private details of their relationship private, it was soon revealed that they'd met in 2023, shortly after Kelce went to see Swift in concert on July 26 at Kansas City's Arrowhead

Breaking MTV Records
At the VMAs in September 2023, Swift donned Versace and gabbed with Ice Spice. By the end of the night she'd made history for the most wins in one ceremony, scooping up nine of the signature astronaut trophies.

Stadium, the site of his NFL day job. Kelce said that he tried to meet the singer after the show (which he has so far seen an additional 13 times) and that he even had a friendship bracelet decorated with his phone number that he wanted to slip to her. But that wasn't to be. Two months later, during an interview on *The Pat McAfee Show,* Kelce admitted that he had invited Swift to watch a Chiefs game, telling her: "I've seen you rock the stage at Arrowhead [Stadium]. You might have to come see me rock the stage at Arrowhead and see which one's a little more lit." It was hardly a Shakespearean sonnet, but the ball had been placed squarely in Swift's field, as it were, and she was ready to play. "Travis very adorably put me on blast on his podcast, which I thought was metal as hell," she said. "We started hanging out right after that. So we actually had a significant amount of time that no one knew [about], which I'm grateful for, because we got to get to know each other."

On Sept. 24 of that year, Swift appeared in Kelce's private box at Arrowhead for a game against the Chicago Bears, cheering alongside Kelce's mother, Donna. Afterward, Swift and Kelce were seen leaving the stadium together. They would end up at a restaurant that he had rented out, where she spent time with his friends and family. Vague non-denials and obfuscations emanated from Swift's camp about

how the two were "having fun" and "hanging out." But the following Sunday, Swift was back in a private box at New Jersey's MetLife Stadium alongside Mama Kelce and some of the singer's A-list plus-ones, including Sabrina Carpenter, Hugh Jackman, Blake Lively, Antoni Porowski, Ryan Reynolds and Sophie Turner. The cat was out of the bag.

From that point on, the NFL broadcasters seemed as interested in capturing close-ups of the most famous pop star on the planet in red Chiefs gear as they were with what was happening on the field. Whether you were a teen, a tween or the grandparent of both, the romance took on the epic newsworthiness of such world-famous couples as Liz and Dick or Brad and Angelina. But the new duo didn't shy away

Continued on page 72

She Gets By With a Little Help From Her Friends

This page, clockwise from above: Danielle Haim, Este Haim and Lena Dunham joined Swift for a June dinner party in Notting Hill, London. At the Golden Globes in January, the star caught up with Keleigh Sperry and Selena Gomez. Opposite: Swift went for a pizza in New York City with Blake Lively in January.

'JUST KNOW THAT I APPRECIATE EVERY SINGLE OUNCE OF EFFORT THAT YOU'VE PUT INTO BEING WITH US WHEN THIS TOUR REACHES TRIPLE DIGITS'

—TAYLOR SWIFT, TO THE AUDIENCE IN LIVERPOOL AT THE 100TH ERAS SHOW

Continued from page 69

from the cameras or the attention. And why should they? After all, a huge part of Swift's appeal is her authenticity, and she's always lived her life on her own terms. Why should this be any different? By mid-October she and Kelce made surprise appearances on *Saturday Night Live* and were spotted holding hands during a date night in New York City. A photo of them kissing soon detonated on Instagram.

But, of course, love isn't just about chaste Instagram pecks; it's also about grand sweeping gestures worthy of a Swift song. And Swift would come up with a doozy of a gesture during Super Bowl weekend by jumping on a plane right after exiting the stage of her concert in Tokyo and racing against the clock to arrive in Las Vegas in time to watch Kelce's Chiefs beat the San Francisco 49ers in the big game. After the Chiefs won, Swift and Kelce embraced and kissed on the field under a shower of confetti. It would be hard to script a more fairy-tale moment. And it felt oddly fitting that a couple who had spent the entirety of their relationship under a microscope should have this moment beamed into the living rooms of 123 million people, the most-watched broadcast since the 1969 moon landing.

And yet despite all of the media attention that Swift receives for her romances, it would be a disservice to define such an independent woman and artist solely by her love life. She's also a devoted friend. She racked up an unfathomable number of air miles while crisscrossing the globe on the Eras tour but managed to make time for her closest circle—a group that includes, among others, Selena Gomez, Blake Lively, Zoë Kravitz, Gigi Hadid, Lana

Put Me In, Coach
"You don't realize how big that damn stage is," said Kelce (right, with Swift and the Eras ensemble), who wowed the Wembley crowd with a cameo. "It is easily as big as a football stadium.... It's way bigger than I could have ever imagined."

Del Rey, the Haim sisters and Brittany Mahomes, the wife of Chiefs quarterback Patrick Mahomes.

All the while, Swift and Kelce continued to bond, with trips to the Sydney Zoo and Coachella and even a surprise appearance onstage together in London, when the tuxedoed footballer stunned the audience with a cameo. He'd proposed the stunt as a joke, but Swift was intrigued. He said she asked, " 'Would you seriously be up for doing something like that?' [And] I was just like, 'What? I would love to do that, are you kidding me?' I've seen the show enough—might as well put me to work here." So there he was in late June, beaming behind her at Wembley Stadium during "I Can Do It With a Broken Heart." And despite the song's title, there were zero broken hearts in evidence, only very full ones.

12 TIMES TAYLOR MADE HISTORY

EVEN BEFORE ERAS BECAME A RECORD-SHATTERING PHENOMENON, THE SUPERSTAR'S LANDMARK ACHIEVEMENTS WERE COMING FAST AND FURIOUS. HERE'S A MERE DOZEN HIGHLIGHTS FROM HER MANY REMARKABLE FIRSTS, MOSTS AND BESTS

By **ERIK FORREST JACKSON**

A Grammys Milestone

Over the course of her career, Swift has received 52 Grammy nominations and a whopping 14 wins. But at the 66th annual Grammy Awards in February, one of those awards landed her in the history books. The singer-songwriter's 10th official studio album, *Midnights,* nabbed the award for Album of the Year, making her the only artist to net four such distinctions and breaking the tie she'd held with luminaries Paul Simon, Frank Sinatra and Stevie Wonder. Her previous win, for *Folklore,* made her the first woman to score three awards (before that, she took home the prize for *Fearless* and *1989*). In accepting her trophy for *Midnights,* Swift thanked producer Jack Antonoff and collaborator Lana Del Rey (who had also been nominated, for her album *Did You Know That There's a Tunnel Under Ocean Blvd*) and shared gratitude for an exhaustive list of creative outlets: "I would love to tell you that this is the best moment of my life, but I feel this happy when I finish a song, or when I crack the code to a bridge that I love, or when I'm shot-listing a music video, or when I'm rehearsing with my dancers or my band, or getting ready to go to Tokyo to play a show. For me, the award is the work."

Topping the Hot Country Chart as a Teen

Swift was a mere high school freshman when she wrote "Our Song" for a ninth-grade talent show. It took her all of 20 minutes. She subsequently recorded the track for her self-titled 2006 album, and at 18, she became the youngest artist in history to have written and performed a No. 1 hit on the Hot Country Songs chart. Four more singles from that collection followed it onto the same chart. Surprisingly, "Our Song" landed on the pop chart too. As Swift put it in 2008, "I like to think of it less as crossover and more as spillover." And it was just the beginning of the success floodgates opening up.

Swifties Crash Ticketmaster—and Still Set Sales Records

Fans snapped up 2 million Eras concert tickets on Nov. 15, 2022, the biggest Ticketmaster single-day sale ever. But the "historically unprecedented demand," as Ticketmaster put it, created unprecedented headaches for buyers. Despite the company having instituted a "Verified Fan" program—a faulty attempt to weed out bots that racked up 3.5 million users—visitors to the site encountered crashes, interminable waits and countless snafus. "It's truly amazing that 2.4 million people got tickets," Swift later wrote on Instagram, "but it really pisses me off that a lot of them felt like they had to go through several bear attacks to get them." Sales for subsequent dates, including packed shows in Tokyo (lucky ticket holders, above), proved to be a hair more civil.

The Longest Song Ever to Hit No. 1

"All Too Well," from 2012's *Red,* proved to be a stealth success. "It has a story that is so sacred to me, because... it was my favorite song on the record," Swift said. "I knew that when we put out the album, it wouldn't be a single, it wouldn't be a video—but I knew it was my favorite one." She wasn't alone in those feelings. "The fans just among themselves decided it was their favorite too. They just sort of... claimed it as the most important song from *Red.*" When she rerecorded the set for *Taylor's Version* in 2021, she let "All Too Well" breathe quite a bit more, expanding it from a running time of 5 minutes, 29 seconds to an expansive 10 minutes, 13 seconds. When the new track topped the charts, it made *Billboard* history, overtaking Don McLean's 8-minute, 37-second "American Pie (Parts I & II)," which had held on to the distinction for nearly 50 years.

The Most American Music Award Wins

By now Swift probably needs another home just to store all her trophies and prizes. When it comes to the American Music Awards alone, she needs space for an incredible 40 of the program's Lucite pyramid statuettes, the most wins of all time. Appropriately enough for a fan-voted awards show, Swift pointed to a certain symbiosis with her followers during her 2022 Artist of the Year acceptance speech. Noting that she'd put out more music in the past few years than in the whole preceding decade, she told the cheering crowd, "You made it clear that you wanted to hear [it].... You encouraged me. And so I found that the more music I made and the more music I put out, the happier I was. So I have the fans to thank, essentially, for my happiness."

A *Billboard* First: All 10 Top Spots

Not content to simply claim No. 1s on the *Billboard* Hot 100, Swift expanded her command to claim every single slot of the Top 10 in a single week in 2022. It was the first time in the publication's history that an artist had achieved such a triumph. Drake nearly got there a year earlier, with songs from *Certified Lover Boy* taking nine of the Top 10 places. But Swift's *Midnights* juggernaut steamrollered the rapper's record to land the historic feat. "10 out of 10 of the Hot 100??? On my 10th album???" the numerically conscious star tweeted soon after. "I AM IN SHAMBLES." But there was still more to be shook about: Swift (left, performing "Me!" at the Billboard Music Awards in 2019) bested her own record with the May release of *The Tortured Poets Department,* claiming not just the top 10 slots, but the entire top 14, with "Fortnight" notching No. 1.

billboard

HOT 100

	SONG	ARTIST
1	Anti-Hero	Taylor Swift
2	Lavender Haze	Taylor Swift
3	Maroon	Taylor Swift
4	Snow On The Beach	Taylor Swift ft. Lana Del Rey
5	Midnight Rain	Taylor Swift
6	Bejeweled	Taylor Swift
7	Question...?	Taylor Swift
8	You're On Your Own, Kid	Taylor Swift
9	Karma	Taylor Swift
10	Vigilante Shit	Taylor Swift

Youngest-Ever Entertainer of the Year at the CMAs and ACMs

George Bernard Shaw is often attributed for his adage "Youth is wasted on the young." But that's not the case when it comes to Taylor Swift. In short order she became the youngest person to score Entertainer of the Year at both the Country Music Association Awards (at age 19 in 2009) and the Academy of Country Music Awards (at age 21 in 2011). Attending the CMAs to celebrate her recent release of *Fearless*—which she said she "wrote basically in my bedroom about boys"—she brought her band onstage with her to accept the honor (above). "I will never forget this moment because... everything that I have ever wanted has just happened to me." But there was still more to come—she was onstage once again in 2015 for the ACM's Milestone Award. "I'm so happy, so happy that I learned to write songs in a town like Nashville," she told the crowd, filled with her peers. "I'm so grateful that I learned what hard work is from my heroes who are all sitting here. And I'm so unbelievably proud that I learned [from country music] to treat people with kindness and respect."

Directing Her Way Into an MTV VMA Record

"Every aspect of my job as a singer has affected the way that I am as a director," Swift told the Oscar-winning filmmaker Martin McDonagh during a *Variety* talk. And those highly honed aspects have clearly translated: MTV has bestowed upon the star four Video of the Year awards, as well as three for directing, the most of any female. Among her video wins (pictured at left, from top): "All Too Well: The Short Film" (2021), "Anti-Hero" (2022), "Bad Blood" (2015) and "You Need to Calm Down" (2019), in which she and Katy Perry (in the burger suit) whimsically ended a very public, ahem, beef over the hiring of some backing dancers. "It was really unfortunate," Perry said later on *The Ellen DeGeneres Show,* "but we made amends, and I'm all about redemption and forgiveness and for setting an example for those younger people that it can be cool to ask for forgiveness and confront someone that you may have an issue with or a problem with and talk it out."

Spectacular Streaming Stats

In August 2023 Swift became the first female artist to amass 100 million monthly listeners on Spotify, surpassing other top acts including Rihanna, Ariana Grande and her old pal Miley Cyrus (seen here performing "Fifteen" with Swift at the Grammys in 2009). The streaming service announced the news with a cheeky lead-in, calling it "queen behavior." At the time of Swift's record, the only other act in front of her was the Weeknd.

Bringing Youth (and the U.S.A.) to the Brit Awards

At the 2021 installment of this U.K. music-industry showcase, Swift received the Global Icon Award, becoming the youngest-ever solo artist (at 31) and first woman to be so lauded. She's also the first American to be recognized, joining the esteemed company of David Bowie, Elton John and Robbie Williams. In introducing Swift, *Game of Thrones'* Maisie Williams said, "Her ability to stand up for what she believes in has made her an inspiration to people all around the world." Meanwhile the singer found herself in awe of the actor, who played Arya Stark on the fantasy series. "Anyone who knows me at all knows that *Game of Thrones* is my life," proclaimed Swift. "So the fact that Maisie was here to present this . . . I want to grab you. I can't, we're social distancing!"

Most No. 1 Albums of Any Female Artist

Taylor Swift rained on Barbra Streisand's parade: With the release of *Speak Now (Taylor's Version),* the young upstart eclipsed the recording legend as the woman with the most No. 1 albums. Until then they both had 11, with Streisand holding the title alone. (Meanwhile, on the other side of the gender binary, Swift is tied with Jay-Z, at 14, and lags behind one band, the Beatles, at 19.) Swift has been on a remarkably productive streak, dropping six studio albums in just three years. And Streisand sure doesn't seem like the type to hold a grudge against a powerful, talented and driven woman. After all, the EGOT-awarded star posted the above photo with Swift to her Facebook page back in 2014 with the caption "Chart-toppers!"

Eras Takes Over the World's Cinemas

Perhaps it was no surprise that a filmed version of Swift's financially fortuitous tour would lure masses to the multiplexes. But the haul for *Taylor Swift: The Eras Tour* still stunned: At $261.6 million in earnings for its theatrical run, the 2-hour, 49-minute movie is the highest-grossing concert or documentary film in global box office history. It just squeaked past the record previously held by Michael Jackson's *This Is It,* at $261.2 million. The October premiere of *Eras* was held at the Grove shopping mall in Los Angeles, with 13 of its 14 screens showing the movie. Before the lights went down, Swift (wearing Oscar de la Renta) posed for photos with her band and backup crew, eager superfans and even Beyoncé, whose Renaissance tour was the year's other massive live-show success story. "She's been a guiding light throughout my career," Swift posted on Instagram, "and the fact that she showed up tonight was like an actual fairy tale."

'I'VE NEVER HAD A FRACTION OF THE AMOUNT OF FUN I'VE HAD ON THE ERAS TOUR BEFORE, EVER'
—TAYLOR SWIFT

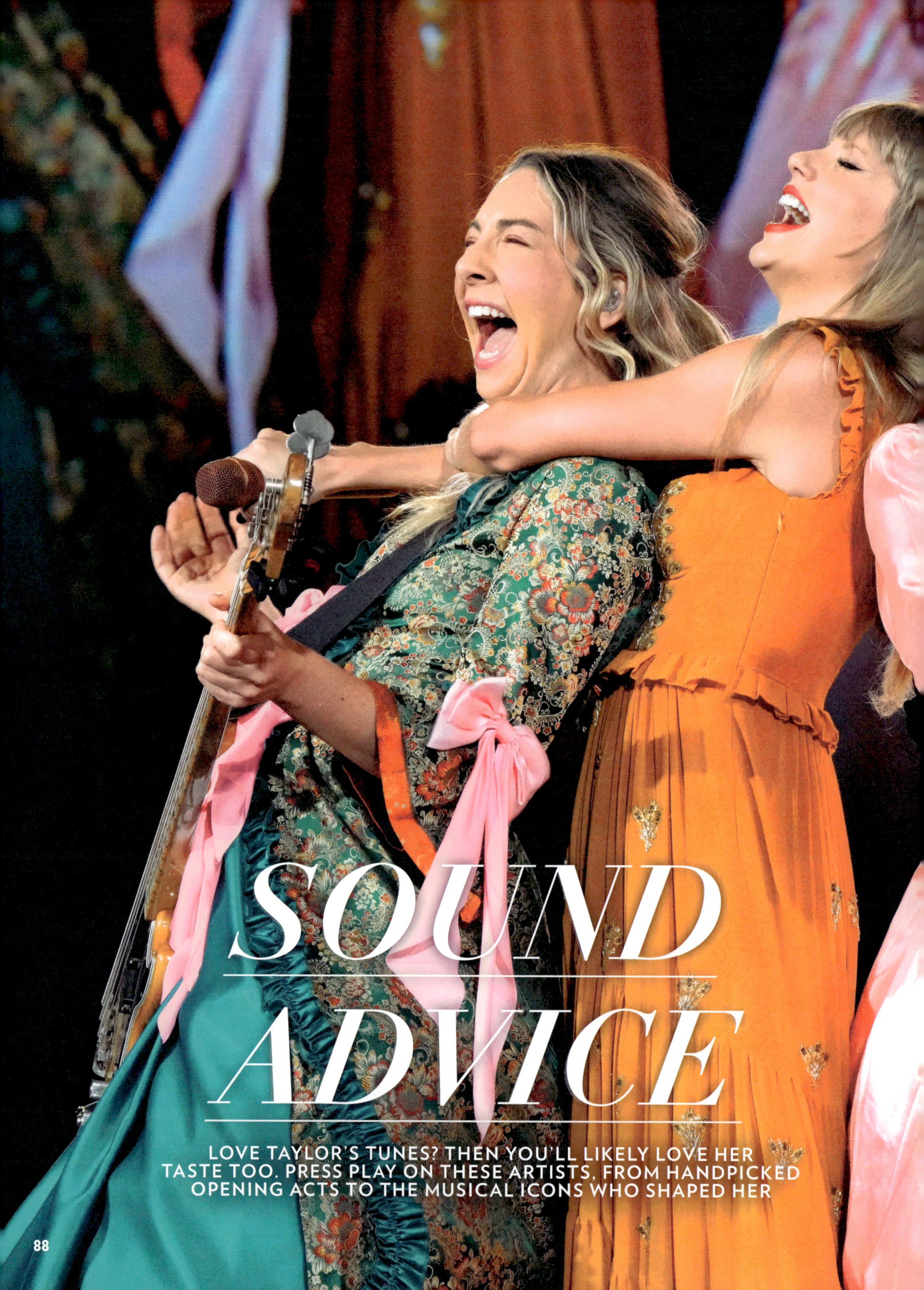

SOUND ADVICE

LOVE TAYLOR'S TUNES? THEN YOU'LL LIKELY LOVE HER TASTE TOO. PRESS PLAY ON THESE ARTISTS, FROM HANDPICKED OPENING ACTS TO THE MUSICAL ICONS WHO SHAPED HER

Haim
On their Eras supporting dates, the pop-rock sister act of Este, Danielle and Alana Haim often joined the headliner onstage. In Santa Clara, Calif., they showed up in costumes that called to mind the ones they wore in the "Bejeweled" video, which Swift directed.

Sabrina Carpenter
The former Disney Channel star's eclectic pop songs grabbed Swift's attention, and the bubbly hit "Espresso" hypercharged many a summer party. Swift calls her pal "incredibly talented, wonderful, gorgeous, hilarious [and] genius," and even brought Carpenter on for a duet after her set in Sydney was canceled because of bad weather.

Beabadoobee

Above: This London indie rocker recalled Swift telling her at the NME Awards, "'Your album [*Space Cadet*] has no skips.'" Her newest, *This Is How Tomorrow Moves*, addresses "entering womanhood." Said the singer: "I just want girls, especially girls, to feel empowered."

Gracie Abrams

Above, right: A Best New Artist Grammy nominee, Abrams went from opening for Olivia Rodrigo to opening Swift's Eras tour. In June she and buddy Taylor released a melancholy duet, "Us."

Paramore

Right: Swift goes way back with the singer of this two-time Grammy-winning pop-punk trio. "Hayley [Williams, right] and I have been friends since we were teens in Nashville," she wrote on Instagram, announcing their tour dates. "I'm screaming????"

Taylor's Musical Icons

Joni Mitchell

Above: Swift's work has often been compared to that of this pioneering folk musician. Speaking about Mitchell's seminal 1971 album *Blue*, the younger songwriter (who perhaps not coincidentally also has an album named for a color) has said "it explores somebody's soul so deeply," including "her deepest pains and most haunting demons." Sound familiar?

Dolly Parton

Left: The beloved country luminary gets Swift's praise as "a legendary empath and the storyteller for the ages," with a sense of humor that "forces the world to reconcile that a woman can be a serious artist and writer who also has raucous fun with it."

Carole King

"The greatest songwriter of all time," proclaimed Swift as she inducted King into the Rock & Roll Hall of Fame in 2021. Swift's parents passed their love of King down to their daughter, who cited the singer's 1971 album *Tapestry* as "a watershed moment for humans in the world who have feelings."

'CAROLE TAUGHT ARTISTS LIKE ME THAT TELLING YOUR OWN STORY IS WORTH THE WORK AND STRUGGLE'
—TAYLOR SWIFT

Tim McGraw
Swift's very first single originated in a high school freshman math class and was named after country royalty McGraw (right). At the 2013 CMA Music Festival, Swift got to perform "Highway Don't Care" with her idol and Keith Urban (center).

Credits

FRONT & BACK COVER
Vittorio Zunino Celotto/TAS24/Getty Images

TITLE PAGE /CONTENTS /INTRO
1 John Shearer/TAS24/Getty Images; 2-3 Kevin Mazur/TAS24/Getty Images; 4-5 Gareth Cattermole/TAS24/Getty Images

INSIDE THE TOUR
6-7 Gareth Cattermole/TAS24/Getty Images; 8 (from top) Kevin Mazur/TAS24/Getty Images; Xavi Torrent/TAS24/ Getty Images; 9 Gareth Cattermole/TAS24/Getty Images; 10 Kevin Mazur/TAS24/Getty Images(2); (from top) Noam Galai/TAS24/Getty Images; Kevin Mazur/TAS24/Getty Images; 12-13 Kevin Mazur/TAS24/Getty Images; 14 Gareth Cattermole/TAS24/Getty Images; 15 (from top) Casey Flanigan/imageSPACE/Sipa USA/Alamy; Kevin Mazur/TAS24/Getty Images; 16-18 John Shearer/TAS23/Getty Images(2); 19 (from top) Marcelo Endelli/TAS23/Getty Images; Emma McIntyre/TAS23/Getty Images; 20-21 Kevin Mazur/TAS24/Getty Images; 22-23 Hector Vivas/TAS23/Getty Images; 24 Mat Hayward/TAS23/Getty Images; 25 (from top) Omar Vega/TAS23/Getty Images; Hector Vivas/TAS23/Getty Images; 26 John Shearer/TAS23/Getty Images; 27 (from top) Taylor Hill/TAS23/Getty Images; Matt Winkelmeyer/TAS18/Getty Images; 28-29 Taylor Hill/TAS23/Getty Images; 30-31 Graham Denholm/TAS24/Getty Images; 32 (from top) Emma McIntyre/TAS23/Getty Images; Kevin Winter/TAS23/Getty Image; 33 Mat Hayward/TAS23/Getty Images; 34-35 John Shearer/TAS23/Getty Images; 36 (from top) Kevin Mazur/TAS24/Getty Images; John Shearer/TAS23/Getty Images; 37 Terence Rushin/TAS23/Getty Images; 38 John Shearer/TAS23/Getty Images; 39 Octavio Jones/TAS23/Getty Images; 40 Taylor Hill/TAS23/Getty Images; 41 (from top) Buda Mendes/TAS23/Getty Images; Natasha Moustache/TAS23/Getty Images; 42-43 Buda Mendes/TAS23/Getty Images; 44-45 Kevin Mazur/TAS24/Getty Images(4); 46 (from top) Kevin Mazur/TAS24/Getty Images; Kevin Winter/TAS24/Getty Images; 47 Octavio Jones/TAS23/Getty Images; 48-49 John Shearer/TAS23/Getty Images; 50-51 (top) Kevin Mazur/TAS24/Getty Images(2); John Shearer/TAS23/Getty Images

IT'S A LOVE STORY, BABY
52-53 Buda Mendes/TAS23/Getty Images; 54 (from top) MEGA(2); Getty Images; 55 (from top) Thomas Kronsteiner/Getty Images; Alex Halada/AFP/Getty Images; Heinz-Peter Bader/AP Images 56 Courtesy Prince and Princess of Wales/Instagram; 57 James Gourley/Shutterstock

ERAS BY THE NUMBERS
58 John Shearer/TAS23/Getty Images; 59 (clockwise from top right) Justin L. Stewart/ZUMA/Alamy; Courtesy BADGER.DOT(4); Graham Denholm/TAS24/Getty Images; Courtesy Tiffany

MAXIMIZING HER MOMENT
60-61 James Devaney/GC Images/Getty Images; 63 Ezra Shaw/Getty Images; 64 (clockwise from top) Gotham/GC Images/Getty; David Calvert/Getty Images; Isaiah Vazquez/Getty Images; 65 Gilbert Flores/Getty Images; 66 Johnny Nunez/Getty Images; 67 (from top) Christopher Polk/Getty Images; Monica Schipper/Getty Images; 68, 69 Kevin Mazur/Getty Images(2); 70 (clockwise from top) Goff Photos; Francis Specker/CBS/Getty Images; Sonja Flemming/USA Today Network/Sipa USA; 71 Robert Kamau/GC Images/Getty

Images; 72-73 Gareth Cattermole/ TAS24/Getty Image

12 TIMES TAYLOR MADE HISTORY
74-75 John Shearer/TAS23/Getty Images; 76 Mark Humphrey/AP; 77 Richard A. Brooks/ AFP/Getty Images; 78 Terence Rushin/TAS23/Getty Images; 79 Christopher Polk/Getty Images; 80 Kevin Mazur/Getty Images; 82 Katherine Bomboy/Getty Images; 84-85 (from top) Kevin Mazur/WireImage/Getty Images(2);JMEnternational/Getty Images; 86-87 John S earer/Getty Images(3)

SOUND ADVICE
88-89 Jeff Kravitz/TAS23/Getty Images; 90 Don Arnold/TAS24/Getty Images; 91 (clockwise from top left) Octavio Jones/ TAS23/Getty Images; Mat Hayward/ TAS23/Getty Images; Frederick Breedon IV/WireImage/Getty Images; 92 (from top) ABC Photo Archives/ABC/Getty Images; Chris Hollo/Opry Entertainment Group and Affiliates; 93 Kevin Mazur/Getty Images; 94-95 Christopher Polk/Getty Images

PUZZLER
96 Shirlaine Forrest/TAS24/Getty Images

POSTER
John Shearer/TAS23/Getty Images; Kevin Mazur/TAS24/Getty Images

PUZZLER ANSWERS

A	L	S	O			C	A	T		O	F	F
R	E	A	R		S	O	R	E		V	A	L
M	I	D	N	I	G	H	T	S		E	V	E
			O	N	T	O		L	O	R	A	X
P	O	E	T	S		S	L	A	M			
E	N	D		T	A	T	E		N	E	W	
G	U	I	T	A	R		A	L	I	S	O	N
	S	E	E		E	S	P	Y		T	O	A
			L	U	A	U		R	E	A	D	Y
S	E	V	E	N		M	A	I	D			
A	R	E		T	I	M	M	C	G	R	A	W
F	A	N		I	C	E	T		E	A	S	E
E	S	T		E	U	R			S	E	P	T

PEOPLE
President Leah Wyar
Editor Wendy Naugle
Group General Manager, Digital Charlotte Triggs
Creative Director Phoebe Weekes
Director of Photography Ilana Schweber
Director of Editorial Operations Alexandra Brez

PEOPLE BOOKS
Editor Allison Adato
Art Director Greg Monfries
Associate Photo Director C. Tiffany Lee
Edition Editor Erik Forrest Jackson
Contributing Art Director Ronnie Brandwein-Keats
Contributing Photo Editor Louis Pearlman
Writers Chris Nashawaty, Kevin O'Donnell
Reporters Mary Hart, Daniel S. Levy
Copy Desk Joanann Scali (Chief), James Bradley (Deputy), Gabrielle Danchick, Rich Donnelly, Shakthi Jothianandan, Dan Morrissey, Matt Weingarden (Copy Editors)
Production Designer Lori Cervone
Premedia Trafficking Supervisor Jacqueline Beard
Premedia Imaging Specialist David Swain
Color Quality Analyst Sarah Schroeder
Production Director Pat McGowan
Production Manager Ashley Schaubroeck
Senior Director of Quality Joe Kohler
Associate Director of Quality Jason Lamb

PEOPLE Public Relations Marnie Perez

DOTDASH MEREDITH PREMIUM PUBLISHING
Vice President & General Manager Jeremy Biloon
Vice President, Group Editorial Director Stephen Orr
Senior Director, Brand Marketing Jean Kennedy
Associate Director, Brand Marketing Katherine Barnet
Senior Manager, Brand Marketing Geoffrey Wohlgamuth
Brand Manager, Brand Marketing Mia Rinaldi

Vice President, Editor in Chief Kostya Kennedy
Creative Director Gary Stewart
Editorial Operations Director Jamie Roth Major
Manager, Editorial Operations Gina Scauzillo
Associate Manager, Editorial Operations Ariel Davis

Special thanks Gabby Amello, Brad Beatson, Nicoleta Papavasilakis

ADVERTISING & BUSINESS DEVELOPMENT
SVP & Group Publisher: Daren Mazzucca (daren.mazzucca@dotdashmdp.com)
VP & Publisher: Donna Lindskog (donna.lindskog@dotdashmdp.com)
Marketing: Sandra Salerno Roth and Christine Austin

Tour de Force

1	2	3	4	■	■	5	6	7	■	8	9	10
11				■	12				■	13		
14				15					■	16		
■	■	■	17				■	18	19			
20	21	22			■	23	24			■	■	■
25			■	26	27			■	28	29	30	■
31			32			■	33	34				35
■	36			■	37	38			■	39		
■	■	■	40	41			■	42	43			
44	45	46			■	47	48			■	■	■
49			■	50	51					52	53	54
55			■	56				■	57			
58			■	59			■	■	60			

across

1 "Furthermore..."
5 Pet seen on Taylor Swift's *Time* Person of the Year cover
8 "Shake It ___" (No. 1 song from *1989*)
11 ___view mirror
12 Achy
13 Actor ___ Kilmer
14 Taylor Swift's 2022 album that swept the Top 10 spots on *Billboard*'s Hot 100
16 Adam's mate
17 "Hold ___ your hat!" (2 wds.)
18 *The* ___ (animated Dr. Seuss film featuring Swift)
20 *The Tortured ___ Department*
23 Close loudly
25 Swift's hit "___ Game"
26 Singer ___ McRae
28 Word in song title "___ Romantics"
31 Instrument Swift played during her *SNL* "Monologue Song"
33 Swift's middle name
36 "___ you later!"
37 Cable sports award
39 Burned ___ crisp (2 wds.)
40 Oahu feast
42 "... ___ for It?" (Top 10 single from *Reputation*)
44 Numerically titled song on *Folklore*
47 Hotel worker
49 "We ___ Never Ever Getting Back Together"
50 Swift's debut single, named for a country music star (2 wds.)
55 Swiftie, e.g.
56 Rapper on *Law & Order: SVU* (hyph.)
57 Relaxed feeling
58 New York's time zone (inits.)
59 Spain's currency (abbr.)
60 Autumn month (abbr.)

down

1 Triceps locale
2 Floral necklace
3 Like breakup songs
4 "Believe it ___..." (2 wds.)
5 Emcee partner
6 Gallery hanging
7 Electric-car brand
8 "Is It ___ Now?" (iHeartRadio Award winner)
9 Type of bean
10 Show off, slangily
12 ___ *Pepper* (abbr.)
15 Swift has 283 million followers on this social app (abbr.)
19 Luxury hotel brand
20 Coatroom hook
21 Burden
22 Falco on *The Sopranos*
24 Big jump
27 Vicinity
29 *"Como ___ usted?"*
30 Lumber
32 Prefix with gram or graph
34 Line from a song
35 Negative vote
38 "Cruel ___"
41 Loosen, as sneakers
43 Rims
44 "___ & Sound"
45 The ___ tour
46 Complain to a friend
48 Paycheck figure (abbr.)
51 Hospital ward (abbr.)
52 Actress Issa ___
53 Egyptian reptile
54 Soggy

By **ROBYN WEINTRAUB**

ANSWERS ON PAGE 95

Made in United States
Troutdale, OR
10/19/2024